THE PENGUIN IN LOST PROPERTY

by Jan Dean and Roger Stevens

Illustrated by Nathan Reed

MACMILLAN CHILDREN'S BOOKS

First published 2014 by Macmillan Children's Books
a division of Macmillan Publishers Limited
20 New Wharf Road, London N1 9RR
Basingstoke and Oxford
Associated companies throughout the world
www.panmacmillan.com

ISBN 978-1-4472-4858-3

Text copyright © Jan Dean and Roger Stevens 2014
Ilustrations copyright © Nathan Reed 2014

The right of Jan Dean and Roger Stevens and Nathan Reed to be identified
as the authors and illustrator of this work has been asserted by them in
accordance with the Copyright, Designs and Patents Act 1988.

3 5 7 9 8 6 4

A CIP catalogue record for this book is available from
the British Library.

Printed and bound by CPI Group (UK) Ltd, Croydon CR0 4YY

No animals were harmed in the writing of this book

For the lovely John – my best thing

(JD)

For Sam, Ruby, Lily,
Merlin, Jasper and Tara

(RS)

Contents

The Penguin in Lost Property

No one will come to claim
the penguin in lost property
because she owns herself.
She is her own penguin
and no one's property.
But she is lost
and can't remember
how she got here.

Things were fine
before the incident
on the ice floe.
She has vague memories:
a killer whale circling,
waves rising, ice rocking, then . . . ?
She rubs the bump on her head
with her flipper.
It's no good, it's all a blank.

She looks around:
a rubber chicken, a blue backpack.
'Right,' she says, 'this won't do,
I've a life to live
and nothing's happening here.'
She waddles to the platform
and boards the Eurostar Express.

Meanwhile, in lost property
there's a row
about looking after *lost* lost property
properly.
And on aisle four,
a small,
significant
and penguin-scented
space.

Jan Dean

Hole

There is a hole
In the space around me
You can't see it
But it goes everywhere with me
It's Border-collie shaped
And it doesn't come when it's called
For it's a hole

It's empty
And it's not called Judy

Roger Stevens

The Perk of Being Mrs Wickins' Cat

There's milk and strokes
and somewhere warm
to sleep and scratch and think,
but the perk of being
Mrs Wickins' cat
is the spider in the sink

The spider's looking scary
and kicking up a stink
So Mrs Wickins calls me. Catch
the spider in the sink

Yes, I'm great at catching spiders,
my claw is lightning fast
I eat the legs one at a time
and save the head for last

There's milk and strokes
and somewhere warm
to sleep and scratch and think,
but the perk of being
Mrs Wickins' cat
is the spider in the sink

Roger Stevens

I Am a Dog

I am a dog
A barking dog
A leaping, growling, barking dog
A wake-in-the-dark, growl-at-an-owl dog
A scary, hairy, growling, yowling, you-can't-get-
   past-me dog

I am a dog
A loving dog
A loyal, licking, loving dog
A squeeze-me-and-cuddle-me, hug-me-and-
   snuggle-me dog

I am a dog
An outdoor sort of dog
A racing-you, chasing-you, outdoor sort of dog
A stick-chasing, stick-chewing, ball-catching,
   fun-loving
Rolling-in-dead-hedgehog-and-fox-poo sort of
   dog

And in case you're not sure
I'm a best-friend, waggy-tail sort of dog
I'm your sort of dog
In short, I'm your dog

Roger Stevens

I Am a Cat

I am a cat
A mewing cat
A howling, yowling, mad-moon cat
A wake-in-the-dark, prowl-on-the-wall cat
A green-eyed, black-furred witch's cat

I am a cat
A comfort cat
A fat-tailed, curve-curled, purring cat
A sit-on-your-lap cat, I'll allow
A long slow stroke along my back

I am a cat
A one-eye-on-the-fishpond cat
A cocked-ear-at-the-birdsong cat
A practise-hunting-with-a-wool-ball cat
A pat-paw-playing, mouse-dream cat
A leaving-a-mole-on-the-mat sort of cat

And in case you're not sure
I'm a don't-care cat
I'll let you look after me, but
I'm my sort of cat
Not an owned sort of cat
Nothing like that

Jan Dean

Oh, What a Din!

Oh, what a din
The *Felis domesticus* and the violin
The *Bos taurus* jumped over the Earth's
   satellite
The small *Canis lupus familiaris* expressed
   mirth to see such jollity
And the eating vessel eloped with the stirring
   implement

Roger Stevens

The Squirrel Speaks

See that dog over there –
white dog, black patch over one eye?
He's my dog
and every day we exercise.
We meet by this tree, him and me,
then it's
dart and scurry
swerve
carve a curve through
the long silk grass
pass that pup by a whisker
frisk then rocket on up
into the leafy layer
to leap from tree to tree.
I am a wriggle of fur
smoky squiggle of fur
swoosh of tail
fat as a grey cloud
fallen from the sky
I fly from branch
to bouncing branch
and every bone in me sings
who needs wings?

He doesn't ever see me make my move.
I can be half a wood away
and he'll still stay
barking at the place I left the ground.
What a completely dopey hound.

Jan Dean

Jenny

The blind dog on the pebble beach
snuffles the grey-green savoury air
cocks her head
to the salt splash of the sea.

The boy in the red jacket
chooses a stone
marks it with a cross
throws it in a high arc
black against the sky
hears it fall. Clatter.

The blind dog by the sea
runs, ungainly,
all lop-sided listening
left ear leaning
to that last limestone chatter.

The blind dog on the beach
finds the place –
hoovers her soft muzzle over the heap
sniffs and sifts the scents
searches
finds the one she knows.

Jan Dean

A New West Side Story

On Seaford beach
The crows are gathering
On the rising shingle
The gulls swoop across the sea
The wind plays the score uptempo
Through the rack and ruin
of the high-tide mark

For now the crows only watch
Hunched in their black overcoats
As the gulls swoop low,
Grey-suited, wheeling and wheedling
Screaming and swearing
And the crows and gulls tussle and tease
But one day
Things will get out of hand
Complicated by one gull's love
For a crow
Crowmeo
And guillemot

Roger Stevens

The Fox on the Beach

The fox ignored us
his muzzle to the salt wind
blowing in from the sea.
Then he upped
and stepped like a prancing horse
paws high and dancey
over sharp mussel shells
till a crab sidled across his path
and his nose dropped
as he eye-to-eyed it.
Then, oh, his jaw snapped
as he snatched that snack
of a shellfish
and hi-diddly high-tailed it
back to his brackeny den.

Jan Dean

Don't

You cannot grab a hermit crab
a waste of time to try –
you know full well he has a shell
he'll hide inside – that's why.

Jan Dean

Pumpkinseeds

We are the pumpkinseeds
Dressed in silver and yellow and blue
The fashion models of the sea
Preening on the catfish-walk
We hang cool
We are not grey and drab
Like the chubby chub or green crab
Who wish they were us

Pumpkins
As you probably know
Are beautiful flowers
That grow on the shimmering moon
And scatter their seeds
Into the ocean home

Even our name
Is rather beautiful
Pumpkinseeds

Roger Stevens

Moon Jellies

Moon jellies, moon jellies
in saltwater sky
gleam white in dark oceans
drift slowly by.

Moon jellies, moon jellies
slow motion glide
swirl in the chop
and rise on the tide.

Moon jellies, moon jellies
notes in a song
sung by the sea
all the blue year long.

Jan Dean

Conger Eel

Swim among
The rotting timbers
Of the shipwreck
Where the ghosts
Of long-dead sailors
Glimmer brightly
Dance upon the quarterdeck
Where shining fish are darting
Like diamonds in the water
As they dive over the edge

But beware the rusting cannon
Where the conger eel is hiding
Its jaws as strong as rusty traps
Waiting for someone to swim by
A crab, a squid, an octopus
Or some delighted swimmer
Distracted by the hornpipe
That still echoes round the windlass
And the capstan
And the kedge

Roger Stevens

Blobfish

Blobfish, blobfish
Deep-sea mover
Sweeps the sea floor
Like a Hoover

Roger Stevens

If Wishes Were Fishes Would I Be a Salmon?

If I could choose, I'd be an elk.
I'd never choose to be a whelk,
a cockle, or a water-snail.
I'd be a whale though, or a quail.

If it were up to me, I'd be a porpoise
but not a slow and shelly tortoise.
I'd quite enjoy the life of birds
or wildebeest in travelling herds.

I fancy being smart and owlish
or even something waterfowlish.
I think it would be quite delicious
to be a shark among the fishes.

Jan Dean

Seashore Sayings

Never fish for crabs by dangling your toes
When eating jellyfish, best use a spoon
Never put a lobster in your pocket, it won't
   like it
When confronted by a seagull, hum a tune

Never make an enemy of any sea anemone
A lugworm will never be your chum
Befriend a sea gooseberry, why not take it
   on the ferry?
And check that barnacles have not stuck to
   your . . . bottom

Roger Stevens

O – Double T – e – R

Otter in the breaking waves
swerves and twists into a turn
her whole body loops then straightens
like joined-up writing in the water.

Otter curls into an **O**
then she ripples and reverses
crosses the double **T** of herself
winds easy to a little **e**
then down up and flick – she's an **R**.

She has magic spelled herself,
a lithe line of gold-brown fur
writing herself in the air.

Jan Dean

Grey Wolf

I am the grey wolf
shadow on snow

I am the silence
of the high places

the dark of ancient forests
I am closer than you know

feel the steam of my breath
in this icy air

see the gleam
the amber lightning of my eye

between black pines
the pack gathers

I am the thunderhead
we are the coming storm

Jan Dean

Stag

Stag leaps,
clears the six-foot fence
with space to spare.

The air moves
full of scents
heavy with information.

Stag stands
within the ruined walls
of Vindolanda
where Romans once walked
and now the tourists come.

Stag stares,
his round brown eye
shines like a dark planet.
I blink, breathe steam
into the cold November dusk.

Stag is antler-crowned
his coat is blood and rust.

He was always here
Is here still.

The Caesars are long gone –
ashes, dust.

Jan Dean

Moose

I am a moose
Like a brick house on legs
Like a deer, but an X-rated version

If I'm in your way
Then, I'm sorry to say
You'll have to go round the diversion

Roger Stevens

Don't Feed the Bears

Look at them. They've ventured from the city
And you're a friendly bear who's stopped to dine
On M&M's. A photo opportunity.
They wonder why the sign says, Bears! Beware.
(Could it be your size? Five hundred pounds
Of power?) And to survive you need to eat.
You open screw-topped tins. You scour the tip
But pickings there are slim. You stroll down
    Main Street
Flick the door latch of a house. You wander
    through
And grab what takes your fancy. Back on the
    road
They're parked up in the lay-by. So you do
Your little dance. You like to work the crowd.
But you remind them who's the boss.
And when the M&M's run out – you can get
    cross

Roger Stevens

*A black bear recently attacked a couple in Canada
when the M&M's they were feeding him ran out.*

Soprano Pipistrelle

soprano pipistrelle
sings impossibly high notes
deep blue
after-sunset-sky notes

so high our ears
can't catch them
but if we could
their song would
be just clicks and plocks

not 'song' at all to us
just noise – a static fuzz
no more music
than a hum or buzz

but I don't think it wrong
to call it bat song

or bat jazz
this is the sound they steer by
as they swerve and sweep the air
in zigzags up above the garden
to hoover up mosquitoes

I watch you
till the darkness seeps
complete
and your fanned silhouette
becomes a part of night

Jan Dean

The Birds in the Forest

The birds in the forest
are green as pears
speckled as trout.

They stare
at the yellow sky
their long needle beaks
suck up the sun
their eyes are black beads
their wings folded close.

They are secret
filling the trees
invisible as leaves
more silent than still air.

There will be no murmuration
no gathering for migration.
They wait
attent
avid

quiet.

Jan Dean

Owl

Stealth bomber
of the kingdom
of birds

Despite
what everyone says
about your wisdom
you actually have
a very small brain

Not that it concerns
the animals
who see your shadow
too late

Roger Stevens

Sad Story

As I was eating ice cream on the prom
a seagull with a very beady eye
swooped down upon me like a feathered bomb
and took my raspberry ripple to the sky.

Jan Dean

I Don't Trust That Chicken

with its head cocked to one side
weighing me up.

I've seen it scratching the earth
with its long claws
seen it stab a wriggly thing
stretch it like gum
drag it up and out
then swallow down
into its own fat featheriness.

I don't trust that chicken
It looks at my fingers
and thinks of worms
plans a peck attack
a beak blitz . . .

That chicken's got its amber eye
on me.

Jan Dean

Bob and Marge

They wandered into our garden
One morning, and stayed
Two cockerels, Bob and Marge

Every morning, while the sun
Was still deciding if it was time to rise
They would start crowing

But they didn't crow
Cock-a-doodle-doo! Cock-a-doodle-doo!
Oh no

Bob would go
Cock-a-gheeek gheeek gheeeeeeek
Erk erk erk eeeuuuuurrrrkkkkkk

Marge would go
Squark squark
Eughueugheuegh gakgakgak

That's how they greeted the new day
It sounded like they were being strangled
It wasn't a pleasant sound

And not really fair on Uncle Bob and Aunt
    Marge
Our Canadian relatives
Who came to visit us

Who didn't want to wake at 4 a.m.
Before the dawn
In the dark

And Uncle Bob never said
Cock-a-gheeek gheeek gheeeeeeeek
Erk erk erk eeeuuuuurrrrkkkkkk

And I never heard Aunt Marge go
Squark squark
Eughueugheuegh gakgakgak

Roger Stevens

What's to Say about Ducks?

All waddle-quackery on land
silk watery-glide afloat
but when the pond is frozen thick
they aren't so slick.

Ducks skate lopsided
fall collided
skid rush and crash
in cold pursuit of crusts
and catapulted crumbs.

Ice clumsies them up
they bobsleigh ricochet
from bank to bank
windmilling their wings
like crazy things.

When winter locks them out
of water
it locks them out of luck –
January's a real bad time
to be a duck.

Jan Dean

Sentries

Three geese sit by the fence
then settle to sleep.
They fold themselves carefully away
snugging their necks and heads
under their white wings
until they are fat oval pillows.

But let a foot step near the gate
and those necks rise
like feathered snakes charmed from a basket.
Then they klaxon,
clatter their wide wings
and holler alarum to the world.
Those yellow bills are hard as horn
those wings can beat to break a bone.

Jan Dean

What Toads Like

A toad will never greet a beetle,
He would rather eat a beetle.
A toad will feast upon a slug
Then for dessert will chomp a bug.

A toad will very rarely heed
The cri de cœur of millipede.
A toad will have a scant regard
For ants found crawling 'cross the yard.

He'll make a meal of dragonflies,
He won't be moved by pleas and sighs.
Grubs and larvae he will swallow
Then in the dark green water wallow.

With one eye on the slow pond skater
He thinks, I'll save that one for later.

Jan Dean and Roger Stevens

Frog

A frog
Still as a stone
Waiting for his supper
A shadow falls across the pond

He's gone

Roger Stevens

Unexpected Affection from an Amphibian

The frog gave me
a bog-hug
a wet and slimy bug-hug

a sticky whip-tongue slick-kiss
a green and licky swamp-kiss.

He clasped me in
a puddle cuddle
a slippy-skinned cold huddle-cuddle
a pondweed in a muddle-cuddle
a quagmire squish-smack fuddle-cuddle.

Did I return his amorous advance?
Not a chance.

Jan Dean

Home for Nervous Newts

In Norris Nutshell's Home for Nervous Newts
You will find
Nigel Newt hiding under a rock
Norman Newt swimming all alone
Narissa Newt reading a book
Nigella Newt cooking a meal for one
And Frank Frog
Wondering how he got into this poem by
    mistake

Roger Stevens

Lizard

Lizard
Quick as a flash
Darting up the stone wall
Sees a shadow in the sky and

Freeze

Roger Stevens

Playing Hide-and-Seek

Hide-and-seek with tortoises
There's lots of time to hide

It's hard hiding from peacocks
As they have so many eyes

Chameleons are quite adept
At finding a disguise

But hide-and-seek with rattlesnakes
Is never very wise*

Roger Stevens

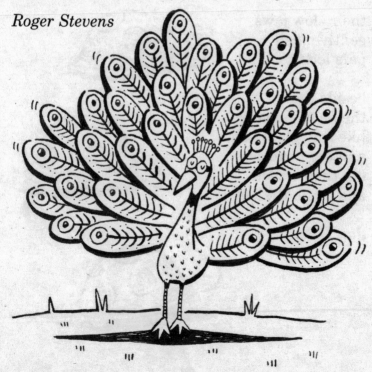

* Although they are quite easy to find if you keep your ears open.

In the Moroccan Garden

in the green shade
five tortoises
doze
eyes shut slits
toes tucked
into shiny shells

when they wake
they are lumbering stones
their claws click
on blue tiles

their slow jaws
gently mash
pale lettuce

beside them
the fountain sings
like tiny glass bells
and the tortoises
dip their heads
and drink the music

Jan Dean

Hedge Pig

Prickle bristle rough as thistle
Hedge pig

Rootle snuffle stomp kerfuffle
Hedge pig

Slug amunch bug acrunch
Curl yourself into a hunch
Hedge pig

Winter sleep – not a peep
Shhh . . . .

Hedge pig

Jan Dean

45

Mole

velvet coat
sharp teeth
spade hand
digs beneath

soil sprays
black fountains
high hills
small mountains

pink snout
seeks worms
bites wriggles
eats squirms

Jan Dean

Unlikely Pets

I have a pet dragon
His name is Dai
But no one ever sees him
Cos he's very, very shy

I have a pet iguana
His name is Stu
I don't suppose you'll ever meet him
Cos he lives in Peru

I have a pet spider
His name is Fred
You can see him if you like
But he's a little bit dead

Roger Stevens

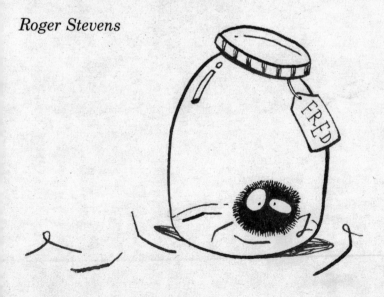

Unsuccessful Pets

Given half a chance
A skink would slink off

In the blink of the eye of a lynx
A skink would skulk away

Yes, I think a skink would slink
Because I once had a skunk

And it slunk

Jan Dean

Herd

All at once
like the tide coming in
the cows run.

From the top of the far field
they gallop
a black and white tide
surging through the hedge gap.

They jostle like waves between rocks
then spread like an opening fan
over the new grass.

Jan Dean

Pig, Disgruntled

She said he was a pig,
but he was not –
he'd no fine trotters
he was no saddleback
no Gloucester Old Spot.

She said he was a pig,
but he was not –
his little nose was not a snout
his ears were small and quite pathetic
his rolling in the mud not energetic.

She said he was a pig,
but he was not –
he was something far less interesting
something boring, something other . . .
it turned out he was just her little brother.

Jan Dean

An Apple for Ash

I stretch my palm into a plate
and offer an apple
polished rosy on my sleeve.

She trots to the gate
arches her dark neck
and takes it – delicate as a fine lady
lifting sugar lumps with silver tongs.

I watch her chew –
not an up and down movement
like a human being
but a sideways swivel. Strange.

I feel her warm pink breath
stroke the silk and whiskeriness
of her lovely nose.

Listen to her whicker and softsnort
the pad of her hoofs
on the damp earth.

Her eyes are roundbrown
gentle, her shoulders sleek,
her mane a dark fall.
She wears the sky like a crown.

Jan Dean

Cows

Cows rarely gaze at the sky
And wonder why it's so blue
But they stare at the ground
Sort of mooching around
And they chew and they chew
And they chew

Roger Stevens

The Flocks of Lochaline

My neighbours are sheep,
they leave me wool on the fence
and save me the trouble of mowing the grass.

When I pass them
they don't wave or nod,
they watch me
from the corners of their yellow eyes.

Today I saw them step dainty
on the cattle grid,
toe-tip-toe on each spaced bar,
balancing steady as tightrope walkers,
crossing that barrier
meant to keep them in . . .

Now they laze in the road by the loch
defying the drivers in their cars.
Won't shift.

Jan Dean

Woodworm

Oh, woodworm
So busy
So small
Your calling card a thousand grains
    of pepper
Spilt on the floor
Sure
Your diet
Is a challenge to humans
But I'm with Noah
I'm on your side
You were a pair when you boarded the ark
A thousand when you disembarked
But you didn't eat the floor
Of the boat, did you?
No!

So, living with you
Will be a challenge
But we'll cross that wooden bridge
When we come to it

Roger Stevens

Midges

we snuggle
all winter in soft brown peat
warm in the moss
we dream of meat

we rise
in the spring and hang in the air
by water or hedge-gap
you'll find us there

we hover
wherever you must wait
we ambush and bite
as you open the gate

we feed
as you fumble to open the latch
suck sweet sips of blood
when we've finished . . . . you'll scratch

and you'll scratch, and you'll scratch

Jan Dean

Mosquito

Oi
Mosi

Quit,
Mosi,
Quit!

Roger Stevens

No Flies on This Poem

To be accurate
A true fly
Has a single pair of wings
Like houseflies and fruit flies
And many flies that bite or sting
Like hoverflies and horseflies
And mosquitoes, flies that bite you
In your beds

Then there are thick-headed flies
(They have big heads)
And small-headed flies
With . . . can you guess?
Yes, small heads.
Long-legged flies
Have got . . . that's right!

And midges are called sandflies
Punkies and no-see-um flies
And let's not forget
Bluebottles and blowflies

Orange flies (or thricops)
(I'm getting bored
It's time to stop)

But I'll just mention
The soldier fly
Who wears stripy suits

Carries a gun
And wears big boots
Oh my, there must be
A hundred thousand different flies
And I must admit
I can't disguise
My favourite animals
Are not flies

Roger Stevens

Beetly Bug

Hey little beetly bug
Crawling up my fingertip
Wonder why you never slip
Wonder how you get a grip

Hey little beetly bug
In your world so teeny wee
Probably you can't see me
I may as well just be a tree

Roger Stevens

I Had a Pet Worm Once

I had a pet worm once,
and kept him in a jar,
without those glass walls round him
he would have wriggled far,
far into the soft black soil,
far beneath the ground,
he'd have tunnelled to Australia
or been New Zealand bound.

I had a pet worm once,
and I let him out to squirm,
all pink upon the tickly grass,
my long and lovely worm . . .
but then he dipped into the earth
like a swimmer in the sea
and that's the last I saw of him
and the last he saw of me.

Jan Dean

What Am I?

Hide and seeker
Pattern maker
Silent watcher
Patient waiter

Crevice haunter
Beetle catcher
Deadly hunter
Fly dispatcher

Venomous biter
Silk-wrap spinner
Pull it tighter
What's for dinner?

Roger Stevens

A spider.

The Natural History of Our Shed

Shiny as a drop of treacle,
dogged straight-line-trundling beetle
creepy-crawls across the floor
and disappears beneath the door.

Woodlice round as bowling balls
curl in the cracks where floor meets walls.
Old webs hang grey and sad as sighs
studded with the husks of flies.

Silver-ribbony rivering trails
lead to three firmly suckered snails.
So form a neat and tidy queue
and come into our garden zoo.

Jan Dean

I Caught a Grasshopper

I caught a grasshopper –
heard its sawtooth squeaky song
then let my eyes follow my ears
to the pale blade where it sat
moved soft and slow
so that it wouldn't know that I was there
cupped it in my hands
before its hairpin legs could flick
and bounce it far away.

I caught a grasshopper –
felt it tickle in my pink palms.
Gotcha. Laughed.
But what can you do
with a grasshopper?
What use is a grasshopper
without the field,
without the sky?
How can it be a green scratch
against the blue
if you don't let it leap?

So I opened the box of my fingers –
it wasn't mine to keep.

Jan Dean

A Walk in Bédoin

A pale sphere of softest mauve
And sharp the thistle thorn.
A butterfly of black and yellow
Darts
Now here, now gone

With eyes and face upon his tail
A smile or a frown?
Wings wrapped, eyes closed.
A withered leaf
On grasses burnt and brown

Roger Stevens

Wasp

In my black and yellow stripes
I'm pure pizzazz.
I am snazzier than snazz –
my wingbeat buzz
is insect jazz.
Birds sing – I do my thing,
my wild electric fizz and zing.

I sting.

Jan Dean

Fly

I
Am only
A fly

Misunderstood
Am I

I am not selfish
Like the mosquito
After your blood

Or aggressive
Like the wasp
In a bad mood

Not a scary surprise
Like a croc
In the mud

Or secretive
Like the beetle
Quietly snacking on wood

Or needy
Like a beagle
Clamouring for food

Or boring
Like a sloth
So quiet and subdued

Or scary
Like a rhino
With a bad attitude

All I want
Is a little food
A mate
Some warmth
Some love
If only I knew
Why you
Persecute me?

I
Am only
A fly

Roger Stevens

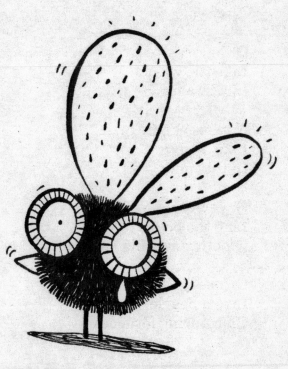

The Funnel-Web Spider

The Australian funnel-web spider
Hides in the loo
And will bite your bottom
When you go for a call of nature

Roger Stevens

The Bees of London

London bees
Are good-tempered bees
And they live in the parks of London

They are quiet and polite
And they always say please
The bees in the parks of London

And these bees make no fuss
They create quite a buzz
For the folks in the parks of London

Everyone loves the hum
And the sweet harmonies
Of the bees in the parks of London

Roger Stevens

Thorny Devil

I'm a thorny devil
A kind of spiny reptile
Who loves ants

I can eat up to six thousand ants
In one meal
I love ants

I can eat them at the rate of
Forty-five ants a minute
I love ants

I eat them one delicious morsel
At a time
Because I love ants

Yes, I'm a thorny devil
I don't suppose you have any ants, do you?
I'm feeling peckish

Roger Stevens

The Lions in the Garden

the sun has sucked their yellow wood to silver
ice and snow have cracked the grain

and we have weathered them too
smoothed their muzzles with unnumbered
    strokes

one sits and stares across the lawns
over red tulips and blue forget-me-nots

the second throws back his head in frozen roar
held in the huge silence of the air

on mad midnights when the moon is red
they rise and leap like fountains

bone and muscle under blazing stars

Jan Dean

Giraffe

You never complain
Do you
With your enigmatic eyes?

Do you think
You are above the mundane concerns
Of we humans?

You have a big heart
The largest of any land animal
For your size

Is that because
You have so much love
To give?

No. It's because it needs to pump
The blood so far
Up to your head

Roger Stevens

In the Lion Park

The lion cub looks like velvet
but feels like doormats,
rough as an old brush.
Pat that fur and dust puffs out,
seems soft – a grey cloud –
but chafes my eyes like grit
and dries my throat.

Now she yawns
opens her lazy yellow eyes
and rests her gaze on me.
What does she see?

Jan Dean

Zebra

First I'd like to clear up
A common misconception
I am a black zebra
With white stripes
Not vice versa

My stripes are camouflage
Disrupting my outline
In the tall savannah grasses

My stripes cause confusion
Lions are dazzled by my motion
My stripes are an optical illusion

My stripes are not favoured by flies
Who find them unsettling
Horseflies, the bloodsucking tsetse fly
They stay away

My stripes have a unique pattern
A kind of barcode of the bush
And though I may not always remember your
   face
I will always remember your stripe

Roger Stevens

Meeting a Monkey

At the monkey sanctuary
a woolly monkey looked at me.

She picked her way so carefully,
tiptoed, then sat upon my knee.

She took a peanut from my hand,
her fingers warm as silky sand.

Her eyes were brown and round as grapes,
her fur was curled in sheepy shapes,

soles of her feet were tender, soft.
She stood and stared then leaped aloft

and swung in the leafy, spreading tree,
chattering and gazing down at me.

Jan Dean

Monkeys

Emperor tamarin
Swinging through the trees of Brazil
Named after the German emperor Wilhelm II
With your elaborate white moustache

White-faced saki monkey
Your thoughts are well hidden
Behind that mask

Proboscis monkey
I wonder what you are thinking
Probably – 'Hey, don't I look the most
   handsome monkey
You ever saw?
Don't you love my magnificent nose?'

Roger Stevens

with your thick skin, **R**ugged bad-guy looks
in Africa and Sumatra two **H**orns. In Java
and in **I**ndia you have one
odd-toed ungulate, **N**ervously disposed
you are a **O**ne-ton heavyweight
in the bush we heard a **C**rash of you
you are **E**ndangered, fools believe
your ho**R**n will relieve the fever
you are an **O**rnery creature
but the most **S**ensitive of beasts

Roger Stevens

Crocodile Tears

They say that
Crocodile tears
Are not real tears

Yet surely
Once in a while
A crocodile
Will be sad?

But then
How would anyone know?

Roger Stevens

Panda

Good morning panda
How are you?
I see you're munching
On bamboo

But for a change
Why not try stew?
Some lettuce leaves
A nut or two?

Fine dine on pike
Or caribou
On fancy plates
As cordon bleu?

For variety
A cheese fondue
With Wensleydale
Or Danish Blue?

But all you do
Is chew bamboo
It's such a boring
Thing to do.

Although I've heard
If you can grab it
You're rather partial
To a rabbit

Roger Stevens

A panda's diet consists almost entirely of bamboo and, because it has so little nutritional value, it will eat between twelve and thirty-eight kilos a day of the stuff. Occasionally, though, it will eat a pika, which is a small mammal of the rabbit family.

The First Elephant of Spring

In March the circus comes
and elephants are on the heath.
They graze on bales of hay
winding their trunks around the stems
like thick grey scrolls around gold threads.
Their paddock is marked out
by iron stakes and taut ropes
but they come to the edge
lean their huge heads towards us
hoping for carrots.
We look at each other
their eyelashes stiff as bristle
skin strangely freckled and folded
wrinkles deep as grooves cut into wood.
The one called Abha nudges me
I rest my hand on her forehead
and she is warm
so warm . . .
I was not expecting that.

Jan Dean

High Street Hippo

I met a hippopotamus once
just outside Boots the Chemist.
He was having trouble
with the double doors
which were stiff and awkward.

He was stiff and awkward too
and needed muscle rub
and moisturiser
and a better brand of toothpaste.

He caused a bit of stir
and a bit of a falling down –
aisle two and aisle three
are kind of one thing now
and there was this small stampede
to the back of the store –

I could just see the pharmacist's feet
dangling from the skylight
as she made it up the shelves and out.

I got my paracetamol
and put my money on the counter.
'Don't buy that bubble bath,'
I told the hippo,
'it'll run to nothing in a river.'
He saw my point.
We left.

Jan Dean

Slug

lover
of the dark
and
damp
this poem
is for
you

exposed
to the light
you
feel
the
danger

fear the sharp beak
the sniffly snout

the little poem
I've written for you
will feel safer
inside this book
hidden away
in the
dark

reader, turn the page
quickly
close the book now
please

Roger Stevens

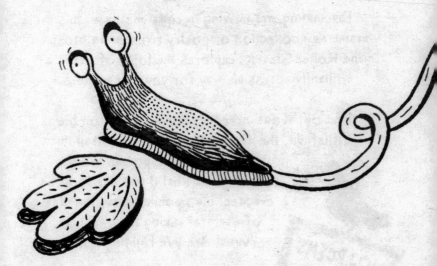

What Are We Fighting For?

BRIAN MOSES AND ROGER STEVENS

Fascinating and moving in equal measure, this brand-new collection of poetry from Brian Moses and Roger Stevens explores the topic of war in a brilliantly accessible way for younger readers.

Find out about incredibly brave animals on the battlefield, the day soldiers played football in no-man's-land, poems about rationing and what it was like to be an evacuee, plus poems about the idea of warfare, asking the question What Are We Fighting For?

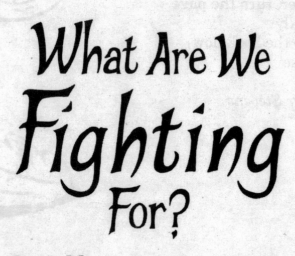

NEW POEMS ABOUT WAR